CW01431817

Original title:

Whispers of the Eternal Labyrinth

Copyright © 2025 Swan Charm

Author: Sebastian Sarapuu

ISBN HARDBACK: 978-1-80561-291-9

ISBN PAPERBACK: 978-1-80561-852-2

Revelations in the Spiraling Shadows

In the depths where whispers weave,
Shadows dance as secrets grieve.
Light breaks through the darkened haze,
Revealing truths in winding ways.

A silent call from deep within,
Guides the heart, where dreams begin.
Each step echoes, a heartbeat's song,
In spiraling shadows, we belong.

Beneath the veil of silent night,
Glimmers of hope ignite the sight.
Each flicker shows what once was lost,
In the shadows, we bear the cost.

Whirlwind thoughts twist and twine,
Carving paths, both yours and mine.
Through the chaos, visions break,
In the shadows, we choose our fate.

The journey bends, but never ends,
With every turn, the past transcends.
In revelations, we find our peace,
Embracing shadows, we seek release.

The Cryptic Map of Lost Journeys

On parchment worn and edges frayed,
A journey waits, a path well laid.
With compass lost and dreams in tow,
We navigate the tales of woe.

Each mark a place where hearts once bled,
A treasure trove of hopes long dead.
Through valleys deep and mountains high,
We seek the truth beneath the sky.

A cryptic code in every curve,
The secrets hidden, we must serve.
Unravel time with every stride,
And find the treasures deep inside.

Shadows Dancing in the Maze of Time

In corridors of whispers deep,
Shadows flicker, secrets keep.
Moments weave like threads of night,
Lost in dreams, they fade from sight.

Echoes of a past that sings,
Haunting realms where memory clings.
Time twists through the darkened halls,
While silent stories softly call.

Dancing lights like fireflies glow,
Chasing shadows to and fro.
What was lost begins to rhyme,
As we wander, lost in time.

Ethereal Footprints in the Mist

Through swirling fog where shadows play,
Ethereal footprints drift away.
Each step a whisper, soft and light,
Guiding souls through the fading night.

The mist embraces, wraps us tight,
Taking journeys out of sight.
Ghostly trails of memories past,
In the silence, echoes cast.

Yet hope still glimmers, faint yet bold,
In every tale that's softly told.
We walk the line 'twixt dusk and dawn,
With ethereal dreams to lean upon.

Echoes of the Enchanted Path

Amidst the trees where shadows weave,
An enchanted path, we dare believe.
With every step, a story grows,
In whispers soft, the magic flows.

Crimson leaves fall like gentle rain,
Each a promise, every gain.
Through winding ways adorned with light,
We find our way through day and night.

A symphony of heartbeats blend,
With nature's song, our souls transcend.
On this path where wonders thrive,
We feel the echoes come alive.

The Canvas of Enigmatic Walks

In shadows dance, the whispers sway,
Beneath the moon's soft, silvery ray.
Footprints trace a tale of yore,
Unfolding secrets on sandy shore.

Colors bleed where dreams align,
Each brush a story, each line divine.
The world spins in curving arcs,
In the night, igniting sparks.

We wander lost on winding ways,
Seeking truths the heart betrays.
Every path a hidden song,
Entwined in echoes, we belong.

Gaze upon the canvas wide,
With every step, a choice to bide.
In the gallery of soul's embrace,
We find our rhythm, our sacred space.

Searching for Clarity in a Twisted Fate

In foggy dreams where shadows crawl,
A labyrinth weaves, both grand and small.
Threads of fate, they twist and bind,
Lost in the maze, the heart's designed.

Glimmers of light through serrated haze,
Guide the way through this tangled maze.
Questions linger, what is true?
Searching for answers, just me and you.

Every corner holds a chance,
To break the cycle of fate's dance.
Hope whispers soft in tangled lines,
Clarity waits where fate entwines.

With weary feet, we roam the scene,
In the chaos, seek what's been unseen.
Ink spills stories on paper's shaped,
We navigate pathways engraved.

The Maze Where All Paths Converge

In a realm where all roads meet,
Time and space dance to a beat.
A crossroads carved from dreams and fears,
Echoing laughter, resonating tears.

Choices linger at every turn,
Lessons learned, the heart must yearn.
Each path a journey, a unique tale,
Through whispers of wind, we set sail.

Lost in the weave of fate's embrace,
Every turn, a new face.
In this maze, we find our core,
Unlocking doors to realms of lore.

Together we walk, hand in hand,
Navigating this shifting land.
As paths converge and stories blend,
In the maze, we'll find our end.

The Eternal Throughway of Secrets

On a highway of whispers, we glide,
With echoes of the truth as our guide.
Beneath starlit skies, shadows play,
Each mile reveals what words can't say.

The road is long, a winding thread,
Through valleys where silence dreads.
Veils of mystery draped in night,
Hiding wonders from our sight.

Footsteps mark the sacred ground,
In every silence, a truth is found.
The secrets held in twilight's glow,
Flow like rivers where dreams freely go.

With every turn, a tale unfolds,
Of stories whispered, of legends told.
In the warmth of dusk, we travel still,
Seeking the heart of life's deep thrill.

Illusions in the Forgotten Labyrinth

Whispers in shadows linger deep,
Echoes of secrets lost in sleep.
Winding paths twist and turn,
In tangled webs, the soul will burn.

Mirrors reflect the dreams we chase,
Fragments of time in a hidden space.
Reality bends, a fragile thread,
In corridors where hopes are wed.

Faces fade in the dim-lit maze,
Each step forward a fleeting gaze.
Labyrinthine routes, so profound,
Where silence reigns and truths are drowned.

Flickering lights guide weary minds,
But clarity is what fate blinds.
In this parting of dusk and dawn,
The heart's desire lingers on.

Lost in the depths where shadows play,
The mind seeks solace, but drifts away.
In this forgotten place we roam,
Illusions carved—forever home.

The Dance of the Endless Turns

Spinning wheels in the moon's soft glow,
A rhythm of time, a constant flow.
Each step forward, a step in place,
The dance of life—an endless race.

Curved paths weave like a lover's glance,
Every heartbeat is part of the dance.
Step by step, the journey's embrace,
In a whirl of joy, we find our space.

Round and round, the world spins free,
Echoing laughter fills the spree.
With every turn, we lose, we gain,
Yet in this dance, no one feels pain.

Fleeting moments in a twirling blend,
The cycle of life has no clear end.
In the silence between each twine,
Together we move, sacred, divine.

As twilight fades into the night,
We lose ourselves in the dance of light.
Endless turns beneath the skies,
Where every soul is meant to rise.

A Tapestry of Uncharted Routes

In woven paths where dreams collide,
Colors merge, no need to hide.
Each thread a story, rich and bold,
A tapestry waiting to be told.

Crossroads beckon with silent grace,
Inviting hearts to find their place.
Every twist reveals a new door,
Adventures waiting on the floor.

Maps unknown in the mind's domain,
Calling forth joy and whispering pain.
In the fabric of life, we stitch and seam,
Unraveling paths like a fleeting dream.

With open eyes, we seek to find,
The lost routes of our wandering mind.
In every choice, let colors merge,
A tapestry where spirits surge.

Embroidered tales of laughter and strife,
In uncharted routes, we shape our life.
Together we weave through hope and doubt,
A dance of fate, both lost and found.

The Call of the Obscured Horizon

Far beyond where the eye may see,
Lie whispers of what is meant to be.
Horizons framed in misty light,
Call to the dreamers of the night.

Veiled secrets dance on the breeze,
Promises linger among the trees.
With each dawn, a new chance grows,
As shadows fade, the calling flows.

In twilight's grasp, we long to stride,
Towards the horizon, the great divide.
Where hearts entwine and spirits soar,
In the unknown, we seek for more.

The canvas blends in hues of dawn,
With every breath, a new path drawn.
Each star a guide, a sign, a clue,
To venture forth, to seek the true.

The call resounds, both soft and clear,
Urging us to venture near.
In the distance, dreams awaken wide,
To the obscured horizon, we will glide.

Quest for the Elusive Map

In shadows deep, the whispers call,
A journey waits beyond the fall.
With lanterns bright, we seek the way,
To find the map of yesterday.

Through tangled woods and rivers wide,
We chase the dreams that fate has tied.
Each step an echo, a tale untold,
Of treasures lost and legends bold.

The compass spins, the stars align,
In search of secrets, we entwine.
With courage high, we face the night,
The map awakens with ancient light.

As dawn arrives, the mist will fade,
In every heart, a memory laid.
We hold the map, our spirits soar,
The quest continues, forevermore.

The Serpent's Dance in the Dark

In shadows slithering, a tale begins,
The serpent dances, the night it spins.
With every sway, the silence breaks,
A rhythm whispers, the darkness shakes.

Underneath the moon's soft glow,
Its scales shimmer, a mystic flow.
It coils and twists in a secret trance,
Inviting all to join the dance.

Echoes of ages, forgotten lore,
In every motion, there's so much more.
The night draws near, a spell so sweet,
Under its charm, we move our feet.

With eyes like embers, the serpent stares,
Entwined in magic, we forget our cares.
In this embrace, time slips away,
The serpent's dance, where shadows play.

Mysteries Drenched in Moonlight

Beneath the stars, where silence reigns,
Moonlight drapes like silver chains.
Each beam reveals a story old,
Of whispered dreams, and secrets bold.

In the garden of shadows, magic blooms,
Awakening hearts in darkened rooms.
With every glance, a tale ignites,
In mysteries drenched in moonlit nights.

The owls they hoot, the breezes sigh,
As secrets linger in the night sky.
Lost in the glow, we wander free,
In this enchanted tapestry.

Glimmers of truth we seek to find,
With every heartbeat, thoughts unwind.
The moon, our guide, so pure, so bright,
In the dance of shadows, we find our light.

Hall of Echoes Beneath the Stars

In the hall of echoes, whispers meet,
Beneath the stars where time feels sweet.
Footsteps linger on ancient stone,
We trace the paths of the unknown.

With each echo, a memory shared,
The voices of those who once dared.
Rich tales woven in shimmering night,
A tapestry of wonder, pure delight.

The sky unfolds, a canvas wide,
Where dreams and fates in harmony glide.
In every corner, mysteries old,
Breathe life to stories forever told.

As starlight dances, so do we,
In the hall of echoes, wild and free.
With hearts united, we find our way,
Guided by echoes, come what may.

Labyrinthine Dreams in Twilight's Grasp

In twilight's hush, the shadows crawl,
A maze of thoughts where echoes call.
Whispers weave through the tangled night,
As dreams take flight in fading light.

Stars align with secrets deep,
While time forgets and shadows creep.
Footsteps trace a winding path,
In this realm where shadows laugh.

The moon unveils a hidden door,
To realms untouched, forevermore.
Lost in spirals of the mind,
What treasures here are yet to find?

Nebulous forms twist and twirl,
As thoughts unfurl in a mystic swirl.
Through corridors of silence roam,
In labyrinthine dreams, we find our home.

Secrets Hidden in a Twisted Journey

Beneath the surface, shadows play,
In twisted paths where lost truths stay.
A journey fraught with twists and turns,
As flame of knowledge brightly burns.

Veiled in mystery, the whispers stay,
The tales of old lead us astray.
Yet through the dark, a light does shine,
Illuminating the path divine.

With every step, a secret learned,
Of paths unmet and pages turned.
A tapestry of fate unwinds,
Revealing threads of tangled minds.

In silence spoken, the truth is found,
Amongst the shadows that dance around.
We wander forth through fog and mist,
On this journey of the secrets kissed.

The Cipher of Celestial Paths

Stars are guides on the skyward sea,
Whispering truths, both wild and free.
In the void where silence reigns,
A cipher reads through cosmic chains.

Celestial bodies spin and play,
Decoding dreams in a grand ballet.
Galaxies swirl with secrets deep,
In the embrace of the starry keep.

Asteroids hide in shadow's thrall,
While comets blaze with a fiery call.
Constellations map the soul's retreat,
In this dance, the heart's pulse beats.

Lost in time, yet never alone,
The universe sings in a cosmic tone.
In every turn, a pattern drawn,
In the cipher's grace, we are reborn.

Embracing the Infinite Unraveling

Embrace the void, where whispers dwell,
An infinite tale, too grand to tell.
With each unraveling thread we find,
A path uncharted, by fate entwined.

In silence, echoes of dreams arise,
Reflections dance beneath the skies.
With hands outstretched, we seek the light,
Amidst the dark, our hearts take flight.

Truths emerge like stars anew,
In the embrace of the vast and true.
Through every turn, our spirits soar,
Together, we seek forevermore.

Infinite journeys bend and twist,
In the fabric of time, we persist.
Embracing life as threads unwind,
In endless loops, our hopes aligned.

Navigating the Veiled Domain

In shadows deep, where whispers fade,
A path emerges, quietly laid.
Each step I take, a secret tread,
Through veils of silence, softly spread.

A flicker of light, a distant call,
Guides me gently through the thrall.
With every turn, the unknown grows,
In this domain, where no one knows.

The air is thick with ancient tales,
Of wanderers lost in misty gales.
I grasp the threads of fate's design,
In this veiled world, my heart entwined.

Each choice I make, a delicate thread,
Navigating fears, where angels tread.
A dance of shadows, a fleeting light,
In the domain where day meets night.

The journey unfolds with each new sign,
Guiding my soul to realms divine.
In veils of mystery, truths emerge,
I navigate this quiet surge.

The Harmony of Entwined Fate

In silent echoes, our fates align,
Two souls united, a dance divine.
With every heartbeat, the rhythms flow,
As paths entwine, the currents grow.

A gentle breeze, a whispered prayer,
Revealing love in every layer.
Through trials faced and joy embraced,
Our journey weaves, a tapestry laced.

In stormy skies, we find our peace,
As destinies link, hearts never cease.
Together we stand, both strong and bold,
In harmony's grip, our story unfolds.

With each sunrise, a promise blooms,
In the garden of dreams, our love resumes.
Threads of fate intertwine so tight,
Guided by stars, our future bright.

Through laughter and tears, in every state,
We forge our path, embracing fate.
Two hearts, one rhythm, forever entwined,
In the harmony of love, joy is defined.

Paths that Curve Beyond Time

In twilight's glow, the paths diverge,
Whispers of time begin to surge.
With every step, the stories flow,
Into the night, where shadows grow.

Winding roads through dreams and fears,
Echoes of laughter, traces of tears.
The dance of fate in the moonlight's gleam,
Guides my soul through the timeless dream.

Each curve reveals a hidden door,
A passage to worlds, forevermore.
As moments blend and softly rhyme,
I walk these paths that curve beyond time.

With stardust in my veins, I roam,
In realms where heart and spirit call home.
Through winding trails and endless nights,
Each path I take, my spirit ignites.

Beneath the stars, my journey stays,
A tapestry woven through time's arrays.
In every curve, a truth I find,
On paths that twist and forever bind.

The Silent Song of the Twisted Route

In shadows deep, whispers implore,
A silent song, the twisted lore.
With every turn, secrets unfold,
A mystery in the night, untold.

The path winds on, through branches bare,
Echoes drift with a haunting flare.
Each note a guide, in silence speaks,
To those who seek what the heart seeks.

Beneath the moon, a melody flows,
In tangled paths where enchantment grows.
The twisted route, a lullaby,
Inviting souls to dream and fly.

With every step, a heartbeat strong,
In the night's embrace, I belong.
Each winding turn like a whispered truth,
A silent song of eternal youth.

Through night's embrace, the journey weaves,
Planting dreams like autumn leaves.
In the silent song, my spirit twirls,
Along the twisted route, life unfurls.

The Quiet Call of Endless Turns

In the shadows soft and deep,
Whispers of the past do seep,
Pathways twist, a silent plea,
In the night, there's no decree.

Footfalls light on ancient stone,
Echoes linger, not alone,
Time weaves tales of lost endeavor,
In the quiet, bonds are tethered.

Winds that sigh through leaf and bough,
Carry secrets, here and now,
Every corner turns anew,
In this maze, wisdom grew.

From the stillness, answers bloom,
Guiding hands in darkened gloom,
Watchful stars overhead gleam,
In this journey, dare to dream.

Paths converge as moments blend,
Truths reveal, illusions end,
Every turn reflects our quest,
In the silence, find your rest.

The Labyrinthine Dance of Echoes

In the heart of winding ways,
Footsteps echo through the haze,
Lost in thoughts, where shadows play,
Dancing lightly, come what may.

Voices drift on evening's air,
Fragments of a song laid bare,
In the folds of dusk's embrace,
Eternity finds its place.

Every turn reveals a song,
Haunting notes that linger long,
Whispers weave a tapestry,
Of forgotten history.

Chasing tales through shadowed halls,
Each whisper, every silence calls,
Guided by the pulse of night,
In the labyrinth, seek the light.

Echoes dance in timeless grace,
Leave behind a fleeting trace,
In this maze of past and found,
Feel the magic all around.

Songs of the Timeless Journey

Across the ages, stories flow,
Guiding us where shadows go,
Every soul a sacred part,
Singing truths from the heart.

Footprints made on ancient ground,
In their echo, wisdom's found,
Every step, a note in tune,
Underneath a watching moon.

Breaths of seasons, soft and frail,
Mark the rhythm, tell the tale,
Through the winds of change we glide,
In our journey, truths abide.

Songs of laughter, tears, and grace,
Woven threads in time and space,
In the silence, voices rise,
Unfurling secrets of the skies.

Across horizons, dreams unite,
Lighting pathways, shining bright,
In the dreamer's heart, we find,
Songs of life, forever kind.

The Fading Light of Forgotten Ways

In the twilight, shadows play,
Memories of a long-lost day,
Flickering like a candle's glow,
Whispers of the winds that flow.

Time leaves marks on weary trees,
Rustling softly in the breeze,
Each leaf tells a tale of old,
In the silence, truths unfold.

Cobblestones beneath our feet,
Hold the stories bittersweet,
Paths once traveled, now obscure,
In the dusk, we must endure.

Fading echoes haunt the air,
Lost reflections, unaware,
Yet in stillness, hope prevails,
Guiding us through shadowed trails.

For every dusk brings forth the dawn,
In the cycle, we are drawn,
To remember what we've lost,
In the fading, gain the cost.

Echoes in the Infinite Maze

Whispers drift through corridors wide,
Lost in the labyrinth, dreams collide.
Echoes of laughter, shadows of fear,
Guiding the wayward, drawing them near.

Twists and turns in every breath,
Dancing around the edge of death.
A flicker of light in the gnawing night,
Hope and despair, a desperate fight.

Mirrored faces within the walls,
Calling from corners, their haunting calls.
Time is a circle that bends and breaks,
Every choice a ripple, every step shakes.

A heartbeat thrums in synchronicity,
Finding a path through the vastness, free.
In this maze where echoes reign,
Freedom is found in embracing pain.

Infinity beckons the brave and bold,
Maps of the heart, the stories told.
Through winding paths, we'll seek the dawn,
In the infinite maze, we carry on.

Shadows of the Timeless Pathway

Footsteps echo on ancient stone,
Tracing the paths where shadows are grown.
Timeless whispers in the twilight loom,
Lighting the way through the gathering gloom.

Each step reverberates in the night,
Illuminating dreams gone out of sight.
Silhouettes dance with a grace profound,
In this endless journey, wisdom is found.

The moon hangs low, a guiding muse,
As we wander the paths we choose.
Memories linger, like mist in the air,
In shadows' embrace, we find solace there.

Branches reach out like arms to hold,
Stories of young and whispers of old.
In this timeless realm that bends and sways,
We learn from the shadows through endless days.

With every heartbeat, we forge ahead,
Carrying dreams on threads of dread.
In the shadows, we glimpse the light,
Guiding us onward through the night.

Secrets Beneath the Celestial Veil

Stars conceal truths in silver winks,
Mysteries hidden in cosmic links.
Beyond the veil where dreams intertwine,
Secrets whisper in rhythms divine.

Galaxies churn with tales so old,
Stories of hearts that dared to be bold.
In the stillness, answers softly gleam,
Under the surface, life's fragile dream.

Planets turn in an endless dance,
Carrying echoes of fate and chance.
Veils of time shatter, revealing the past,
What once was hidden is finally cast.

In twilight's embrace, we search and seek,
Chasing the stars, our spirits speak.
Secrets shimmer in the boundless night,
Under the celestial veil, we find our light.

The cosmos hums a forgotten song,
Carried by stardust, we all belong.
In silence, we feel the timeless thread,
Beneath the veil, we are softly led.

The Veiled Threads of Destiny

In the loom of fate, hands intertwine,
Weaving the stories from moments divine.
Threads of gold, and shadows of gray,
Marking the paths that lead us astray.

Each stitch a choice, a chance to embrace,
Woven by dreams that time cannot erase.
Destiny beckons with whispering sighs,
In the tapestry's folds, our essence lies.

Veils of the future shimmer and sway,
Revealing the patterns in night's gentle play.
Through labor and love, we shape our path,
Facing the storms and weathering wrath.

Yet threads can fray, and paths can shift,
In the fabric of life, we learn to lift.
What's hidden may shine in the light of the day,
The veiled threads teach us to find our way.

As the needle darts, the journey unfolds,
Crafting a fate that in our hands holds.
In every moment, let hope be our guide,
For within the weave, our destinies hide.

Fables of the Gossamer Path

In twilight's glow, the whispers breathe,
Tales of fleeting dreams they weave.
Each step a dance, a story spun,
Through shadows deep, our journey's begun.

Beneath the stars, where wishes rest,
In gossamer threads, we feel the quest.
A labyrinth wild, a heart untamed,
With every turn, a truth proclaimed.

The moonlight kisses the silver dew,
Guiding our hearts, steadfast and true.
Every fable echoes through the night,
As we stroll on paths kissed by light.

In nature's arms, we find delight,
An ancient dance, a sacred rite.
Voices of old, the trees confide,
In fables lost, we take our stride.

Together we roam, hand in hand,
Across the fields, through dream-stitched land.
In the quiet joy, in laughter's spark,
We hold the tales that glow in the dark.

Lost in the Eternal Twists

Where time unfurls like a ribboned stream,
In echoes of laughter, we chase a dream.
Each corner turned, a shadow falls,
In endless twists of fate's own calls.

A tapestry woven with threads of chance,
We wander forward in a curious dance.
The paths we tread, both strange and sweet,
Carrying whispers of souls we meet.

Beneath the stars, we search and yearn,
For every lesson that we discern.
Amidst the chaos, a flicker shines,
Guiding our hearts through tangled lines.

In the labyrinth of dreams we roam,
Each twist uncovers the heart's true home.
With every turn, we strive to see,
The beauty in lost serenity.

Together we dance, 'neath the moon's embrace,
Through turns of fate, we find our place.
In the eternal spiral, we learn to trust,
The winding paths that lead to us.

Whims of the Enchanted Maze

In the heart of the forest, secrets hide,
Where whimsy dances, and dreams collide.
With every step, the magic wakes,
Through an enchanted maze, our spirit takes.

Petals whisper tales of old,
In colors bright, and stories bold.
A journey fraught with wonders bright,
We lose ourselves in joy and light.

Through winding paths, the shadows play,
As we chase the whimsy of night and day.
Each turn reveals a vibrant sight,
Painting our souls in pure delight.

In laughter born from gentle sighs,
We wander freely 'neath starlit skies.
The maze we walk, a dreamlike thread,
Connecting hearts where magic's fed.

Together we search, hand in hand,
In every corner, wonder stands.
In the whimsy of life, we find our way,
Through the enchanted maze, forever we stay.

The Allure of the Unseen Way

In whispers soft, the hidden calls,
Through veils of mist, adventure sprawls.
The unseen way beckons our heart,
With every step, a wondrous start.

Beneath the boughs where silence thrums,
A melody sweet, the heartache succumbs.
In shadows deep, the treasures gleam,
With every breath, we chase the dream.

The path unfolds like petals anew,
Enchanted ground where beauty grew.
With every sigh, we find our grace,
In the allure of this sacred space.

Each moment whispers tales untold,
In the echoes of ages that unfold.
We walk together, through dusk and dawn,
In the unseen way, we are reborn.

Through trials faced and bridges spanned,
We learn the strength of a steady hand.
In the allure of fate's gentle sway,
We find our peace, come what may.

Riddles of the Timeless Traveler

In shadows cast, the secrets lie,
Around the bends where whispers sigh.
A fleeting glance, a sudden smile,
What lies beneath, if just a while.

Time folds like cloth in hands of fate,
With every step, we contemplate.
The paths we've walked, the tales we've spun,
In riddles told, the journey's begun.

A distant star, a guiding light,
Through endless realms, both day and night.
Each choice we make, a thread we weave,
In puzzles deep, we dare believe.

What once was lost may now return,
In timeless dance, the worlds we yearn.
With every heartbeat, echoes trace,
The traveler moves, through time and space.

In laughter shared, in silent tears,
The stories breathe through countless years.
The past, the future, all entwined,
In every step, wisdom we find.

Echoing Dreams in the Unknown

Beneath the stars, in whispered dreams,
Where nothing's quite as it seems.
A call to echo through the dark,
In silent realms, the shadows spark.

Each dream a portal, vast and wide,
With wonders hid where few confide.
In fleeting glimpses, visions swirl,
The unknown beckons, thoughts unfurl.

Through ether soft, where spirits play,
A dance of fate, come what may.
The heartbeats blend, a cosmic song,
In echoing dreams, we all belong.

A tapestry of hope is spun,
In every twilight, new day begun.
With open hearts, we chase the light,
In echoing dreams, we take our flight.

The moonlight whispers, secrets deep,
In tangled paths where shadows creep.
With every breath, we find our way,
Through echoing dreams, mid night and day.

Steps on the Hidden Road

Along the path where silence dwells,
The hidden road, with stories tells.
Each footfall soft on ancient ground,
In nature's grasp, true peace is found.

With every turn, the day unfolds,
New wonders grasped, new truths retold.
The trees, they whisper secrets low,
On steps we tread, the heart will grow.

In morning's glow, the world awake,
With every choice, the course we make.
Through brambles thick, to valleys wide,
On hidden roads, we learn to bide.

The sky above, a canvas bright,
In every shade, both day and night.
With dreams as guides, we walk the line,
On hidden roads, our souls align.

In unity with earth and breeze,
We find our way, we find our peace.
With open hearts, we face the load,
On steps we take, the hidden road.

Echoes of Unfathomable Depths

In ocean's grasp, where darkness sighs,
A realm of wonders, deep and wise.
The whispers carry, soft and slow,
In echoes vast, the secrets flow.

With depths that hold both fear and grace,
Each ripple speaks of time and space.
In currents strong, we are but dust,
In liquid dreams, we place our trust.

The shadows hide what light reveals,
In whispered tones, the spirit heals.
Through fathoms deep, the treasure gleams,
In echoes soft, we chase our dreams.

What lies beneath, we seek to know,
In silent dive, with hearts aglow.
With every stroke, we gain our depth,
In unfathomed waves, we take our breath.

The ocean's song, both fierce and kind,
In every tide, our thoughts unwind.
Through journeys vast, we come to see,
In echoes deep, we're part of sea.

Driftwood on the Celestial River

In twilight's glow they softly float,
Carried by dreams on a silver boat.
Whispers of stars in gentle embrace,
Guiding the lost to a tranquil place.

Each twist and turn, a secret untold,
Stories of ages in driftwood mold.
Ebbing and flowing, a cosmic dance,
Nature's rhythm, a timeless trance.

In the quiet glow of the moonlit tide,
Driftwood treasures, where hopes abide.
Together they sail through the starry night,
On celestial waters, hearts take flight.

The river of dreams, where wishes weave,
Carried by currents, we dare to believe.
Each wooden fragment, a piece of the sky,
Floating in silence, we learn to fly.

Embracing the flow of this cosmic stream,
Driftwood, our anchor, our shared dream.
A journey of love on the celestial sea,
Where driftwood and starlight are wild and free.

The Portal of Infinite Turns

Through twisting paths, the portal calls,
In shadowed echoes, adventure sprawls.
A door of secrets, a passageway bright,
Leading the heart into endless night.

Step through the veil, let the journey start,
With echoes of wonder that tug at the heart.
Each turn reveals what mysteries hold,
Stories of ages in whispers retold.

Time bends and stretches, a dance with fate,
In the realm of the lost, we learn to wait.
Eyes wide open to the unseen flow,
The portal's embrace, a magical glow.

With every corner, new realms unfold,
Tales of the brave and the timidly bold.
Weaving through shadows, we grow and we learn,
In the portal's light, our spirits yearn.

Infinite wonders await at each bend,
In the heart of the portal, time seems to blend.
A voyage of souls in a spiraled embrace,
Forever captivated in this boundless space.

Threads of Time in the Winding Way

In the tapestry of time, we weave,
Threads of moments that we perceive.
Each footstep dances on the road,
Memories linger, a heart's abode.

Winding through seasons, both brave and shy,
The fabric of life gently drifting by.
With every twist, new patterns arise,
Invisible stitches beneath our skies.

Sunlight shines through a canopy vast,
Illuminating the shadows cast.
As we stroll upon this secret path,
We gather the stories, the aftermath.

Threads entwined like the roots of a tree,
Connecting the past with what will be.
In the winding way, our spirits align,
Each heartbeat echoes the threads of time.

With gentle hands, we cradle the fate,
In the loom of existence, we navigate.
Through the cycles of life, we embrace and grow,
In the threads of time, love's light will flow.

Journeys Through the Veil of Shadows

In whispered realms beyond the day,
We roam where light has lost its way.
Through veils of shadows, we boldly tread,
Seeking the truths that lie ahead.

The moon hangs high in the ashen sky,
Guiding our steps with a watchful eye.
Each footstep echoes in the silent night,
Illuminating fears that hide from sight.

Through twisted alleys, lost souls collide,
In the heart of darkness, we learn to abide.
With courage kindled, we face the flight,
Transforming shadows into radiant light.

Journeys unfold in the depths we find,
Mysteries woven in fabric entwined.
Through the veil, we venture to stand,
Unlocking the chains, hand in hand.

As dawn breaks forth, the shadows concede,
We rise from the depths, a heart freed.
In journeys through shadows, we've grown and learned,
In the light of the morn, new dreams are earned.

The Secret of the Arcane Passageway

A door unseen lies deep in night,
The whispers call, just out of sight.
With runes aglow, the shadows play,
Unlock the path, let dreams convey.

Ancient stones recall the past,
Mysteries bound, forever cast.
Echoes dance in twilight's breath,
A journey starts where life meets death.

Beneath the surface, secrets brew,
A key lies hidden, known to few.
Truths rest in quiet, wait to leap,
Through arcs of time, the lost shall keep.

With every step, the silence grows,
In shadowed realms where no one goes.
The air is thick with magic's grace,
Entwined with hopes that dreams embrace.

The flicker fades, the path now clear,
Step forth, dear soul, release your fear.
To find the light in darkest hole,
Unravel all; become your whole.

Layers of Mystery Beyond the Veil

Beyond the mist, a world concealed,
With secrets rich and tales revealed.
Each layer holds a voice unheard,
In whispers soft, the mysteries stirred.

Glimmering light through shadows' touch,
Inviting souls with gentle hush.
A dance of fate in twilight's glow,
Where time stands still, and feelings grow.

Veils of doubt and fear unwind,
In hidden paths, true strength you'll find.
The heart beats strong, the spirit sighs,
Embrace the fog, let courage rise.

From depths of night, the dawn appears,
Dissolving all our doubt and fears.
In every moment, magic waits,
To guide us through the temple gates.

So lift the veil, and look inside,
In layers deep, let truth abide.
Through cracks of life, the light will seep,
Revealing all the truths we keep.

The Labyrinth's Lament

Winding paths through stone and grass,
A maze of echoes, shadows pass.
With every turn, the heart will ache,
As silence falls, a choice to make.

In the center lies a truth untold,
A heart once warm now turns to cold.
The tears of loss, like rivers flow,
And in this place, the sorrows grow.

Footsteps echo through darkened halls,
A distant whisper, a maiden calls.
Through twisted ways, the soul does roam,
In search of peace, in search of home.

The walls are high, yet hearts collide,
In every heart, a truth will hide.
The pain of longing weaves around,
In the labyrinth, hope is found.

So wander far, embrace the plight,
For in the dark, we find the light.
Though lost in time, our souls will mend,
Through every turn, the journey's end.

Temptations of the Forgotten Way

In shadows cast by ancient trees,
Lies a path kissed by a breeze.
With every step, the whispers swell,
A siren's call, a haunting spell.

The road ahead is paved with dreams,
Enticing hearts with silver beams.
Yet danger lurks in every sigh,
For every truth, a tethered lie.

In silence thick, the doubts arise,
Veiled in hopes, a thousand lies.
To tread this path, one's courage sways,
Through shadows deep, where memory frays.

But still we walk, hearts open wide,
Drawn to the unknown, we cast aside.
Seeking a light, where darkness stays,
In temptations of the forgotten way.

So breathe in deep, embrace the quest,
In whispered truths, the heart finds rest.
For every stumble, every fall,
Leads deeper still, to the grandest call.

Lingerings in the Endless Corridor

Shadows stretch and softly creep,
Whispers dance where secrets sleep.
Glimmers fade in muted light,
Echoes haunt the quiet night.

Footsteps lost on ancient stone,
Memories linger, all alone.
Fading pictures, voices blend,
Time unwinds but never ends.

Doors unlatched, yet never near,
Fragments grasped but disappear.
A thread of dreams, a fragile thread,
Weave the tales of those long dead.

Light and shadow play their game,
In this corridor, none the same.
Each turn brings a fleeting chance,
To glimpse the past in waking trance.

All around, the silence sighs,
Beneath the weight of timeless lies.
Linger here, where spirits roam,
In the heart of this long home.

Murmurs from the Forgotten Depths

Whispers rise from caverns deep,
Secrets that the silence keep.
Rippling waters, shadows play,
Murmurs call from far away.

Stalactites hang like frozen tears,
Voices tremble with ancient fears.
In the dark, lost stories sigh,
Echoes drift on currents high.

Silent echoes, tales untold,
Of lives once vibrant, bold and gold.
In this realm, the past exists,
Among the stones, in twilight mist.

Flickering lights, a phantoms' song,
In every note, the past belongs.
Murmurs weave through cavern air,
Of those who lived, of those who care.

Here in shadows, memories cling,
With every breath, the echoes sing.
Journey deep where none can tread,
To uncover all that's left unsaid.

Reverberations of the Ageless Spiral

Spiraling down through time's embrace,
Each turn reveals a haunted place.
Resonating with stories old,
In every echo, fate retold.

Winding paths of whispered lore,
Step by step, forevermore.
Every heartbeat, every sigh,
Marks the trails of days gone by.

The spiral twists, the shadows grow,
In their depths, the legends flow.
With every turn, a voice anew,
Calling forth the lost and true.

Time entangled in spiraled dance,
All abide in fate's strange chance.
Reverberate through space and dream,
In the void, the echoes scream.

Journey forth, let go of fear,
In this spiral, all draw near.
With reverberations of the past,
Find the truth that holds you fast.

The Enigma of the Winding Way

Paths entwined beneath the stars,
Finding solace in the scars.
Every bend presents a view,
A riddle waiting just for you.

Winding way, a mystery,
Where shadows dance in reverie.
Markers lost, yet still you roam,
In the depths, you find your home.

Leaves unfurl, the night descends,
A journey where the heart transcends.
Follow whispers, heed their call,
In the silence, hear it all.

With every step, a story wakes,
Unraveled in the path it takes.
An enigma to decipher slow,
In winding ways, the truth will flow.

So wander on, embrace the quest,
In this maze, you'll find your rest.
The enigma holds the world so close,
In the winding way, you'll find your prose.

Chronicles of the Serpent's Path

Beneath the emerald shadows, paths unfold,
Whispers of the ancients, secrets untold.
Each coil of the serpent, a tale divine,
Winding through the ages, where echoes align.

The twilight glimmers, a beckoning call,
Guardians of wisdom, standing tall.
With scales of wisdom, they silently glide,
Through whispers of history, with nowhere to hide.

In the depths of the forest, where mysteries creep,
The serpent observes, in silence so deep.
With eyes like lanterns, it sees what we miss,
Illuminating shadows, an ethereal kiss.

Between the branches, the stories arise,
Of battles and choices beneath the vast skies.
As seasons do change, the path shifts and sways,
The serpent remembers in intricate ways.

So heed the soft rustling, the tales in the breeze,
For the serpent's path flows with ancient keys.
Unlocking the wisdom that dwells in the night,
Guiding lost souls to the dawn's gentle light.

Silence of the Ever-Turning Wheel

In the heart of the night, the wheel spins round,
Where echoes of time in silence abound.
Each tick of the clock, a breath held tight,
In shadows of starlight, fading from sight.

Moments entwined in a dance so slow,
A tapestry woven with threads of woe.
The stillness whispers of what's yet to come,
In the hush of the cosmos, the heartbeat hums.

With each rotation, past meets the now,
The burdens of choices, we silently vow.
Silent as secrets, the wheel does confide,
In cryptic suspensions where sorrows reside.

As hands trace the circle, a journey unfolds,
In silence and stillness, each mystery holds.
The stars bear witness to the dreams we yield,
In the quiet embrace of the ever-turning wheel.

So listen intently, let the silence speak,
For within the void lies the strength we seek.
In the still of the night, let our spirits feel,
The depth of the silence of the turning wheel.

The Hidden Currents of Time

In the stream of existence, currents collide,
Hidden beneath waves, where shadows reside.
The flow of the past through the present does crave,
To teach us the lessons that the waters gave.

Rivers of moments, cascading so fast,
We often forget the treasures amassed.
As ripples dance lightly on the surface aglow,
The secrets of time whisper tales we don't know.

In eddies and whirlpools, we find our own path,
Navigating storms, escaping the wrath.
With every heartbeat, we paddle upstream,
Seeking the truths that flicker like dreams.

As time's hidden currents guide our descent,
We learn from the echoes of what's been spent.
In the depths of the waters, old wisdom does bloom,
Revealing the patterns, dispelling the gloom.

So trust in the currents, let them set you free,
For time flows within, like a deep, endless sea.
Embrace the unknown, let the journey ignite,
In the hidden currents where futures take flight.

Mysteries Weaving Through the Afterglow

In the soft embrace of twilight's warm light,
Mysteries whisper from day into night.
Colors entwined in a tapestry spun,
As shadows and secrets begin to run.

The stars emerge gently, one by one,
Painting the canvas where dreams are begun.
With each flicker and twinkle, a story is shared,
In the hush of the evening, where hearts are bared.

The afterglow lingers, a delicate thread,
Binding the moments when words go unsaid.
As night takes the stage, the mysteries rise,
In the silence and stillness, the universe sighs.

Listen to softly the echoes that play,
In the glow of the dusk, where shadows do sway.
The night holds the secrets the day can't bestow,
In the shimmering dance of the afterglow.

So trust in the mysteries that twilight unveils,
As the world hushes softly, and magic prevails.
In the beauty of silence, and wonders that flow,
We find ourselves lost in the afterglow.

Tracing Threads of the Unknown

In shadows deep, we wander wide,
With whispers soft, the stars our guide.
Each step we take, a secret found,
In the web of dreams that wrap around.

A silken path where fears entwine,
Tracing arcs of fate divine.
Through tangled thoughts, we gently weave,
Unraveling tales we dare believe.

Beneath the veil of night's embrace,
The unknown stirs with timeless grace.
In twilight's glow, our spirits soar,
As threads of life connect once more.

Yet in the dark, the questions hum,
What lies beyond, what's yet to come?
In every heart, a flicker glows,
Pointing to where the river flows.

So let us dance on this unknown strand,
Together crafted, hand in hand.
With every joy and every tear,
We trace the threads that brought us here.

The Cloisters of Ghostly Voices

In cloisters dim, the echoes play,
Whispers of dreams from yesterday.
A spectral tune floats in the air,
Carried softly on memories rare.

Ancient walls adorned with sighs,
Each stone a tale beneath the skies.
Ghostly figures glide with grace,
In this haunted, sacred space.

A touch of warmth, a lingering chill,
Where silence reigns but hearts can fill.
Haunting laughter lingers low,
In shadows where the lost things go.

With bated breath, we pause to hear,
The stories whispered, crystal clear.
In the cloister's heart, time unravels,
As every soul's weight gently travels.

So linger here, in twilight's hold,
With tales of love and fears retold.
In cloisters dark, we find our voice,
Connecting threads, we make our choice.

Labyrinths at the Edge of Existence

In corridors where shadows dwell,
Labyrinths weave a mystic spell.
Each turn we take, the world anew,
At the edge of dreams, where all is true.

Lost in paths of thought and time,
Echoes rise, a subtle rhyme.
Questions linger like whispered frail,
In the maze where stories trail.

Through winding halls of memory's scrawl,
We search for meaning, hear the call.
Each step a dance of fate's design,
In tangled threads, our spirits align.

At the edge, where shadows meet,
The heartbeat of existence, bittersweet.
We brave the dark, our souls a flame,
In labyrinths vast, we seek our name.

So venture forth, embrace the fight,
In the crazy twists, find the light.
For at the edge, we dare to find,
The truth that lingers intertwined.

The Veil Between Here and There

A delicate veil hangs in the air,
Between the worlds, a whispered prayer.
Where dreams take flight on gossamer wings,
In the space where silence sings.

What lies beyond this fleeting haze?
A realm of wonder, a lost gaze.
With hearts awake, we yearn to see,
The bridges formed between you and me.

In the twilight glow, the shadows dance,
Each flickering light a wish, a chance.
Threads of fate weave through the night,
Binding us close, out of sight.

Yet in the stillness, the spirits call,
With secrets that linger, enchanting all.
The veil between holds stories shared,
Of love and loss, the souls that dared.

So tread softly in this sacred space,
Where every breath finds its place.
Between here and there, let dreams unite,
As we wander on, until the night.

Fables Lost in the Abyssal Twist

In the depths where shadows weave,
Whispers of old stories grieve.
Tales of light, darkened by fate,
Lost in the currents, they await.

Echoes of laughter, now forlorn,
Where dreams are shattered, hope is worn.
Each wave a chapter, each tide a sigh,
In the abyss, the fables lie.

Mirrors reflect forgotten lore,
Deep in the void, where spirits soar.
Yet in silence, a truth is spun,
Fables lost, but never done.

Cast away, but never gone,
Each fleeting moment, a fragile dawn.
Weaving patterns in the dark,
Whispers ignite the long-lost spark.

In the maze of the ocean's song,
Fables linger, where they belong.
In the depths, they twist and churn,
Awaiting the heart's return.

Reflections of the Celestial Labyrinth

Stars that twinkle, stories told,
In the skies, mysteries unfold.
Each constellation, a path unseen,
Dancing light where dreams convene.

Galaxies swirl in cosmic grace,
Patterns shift in endless space.
The labyrinth of time and fate,
We wander, curious and innate.

Shadows stretch through the void divine,
Echoes of thinkers intertwine.
Wisdom etched in astral hue,
The universe whispers, born anew.

Moments collide in twilight's maze,
Past and future in a gaze.
Reflections shine in the starlit night,
Navigating by the inner light.

Each step forward, a dance of chance,
In the spiral, we twirl and prance.
Reflections flicker, forever vast,
In the celestial, we are cast.

The Infinite Tapestry Unfurled

Threads of time, woven with care,
In every stitch, memories share.
Colors blend in harmonious swirl,
Life unfolds in a tapestry's pearl.

Patterns form, both near and far,
Guided gently by a silent star.
Each knot a moment, every hue a sigh,
In the fabric of dreams, we comply.

Every story a vibrant strand,
Together we rise, together we stand.
In the weave of existence, we find,
The intricate ties that bind.

Loom of fate, spinning the rue,
Wonders await in the beautiful view.
Endless journey, ever so bright,
Unfurling legends, igniting the night.

As the tapestry grows, secrets revealed,
A lifetime's journey, beautifully sealed.
In the threads we stitch, love and despair,
The infinite tapestry, beyond compare.

Lament of the Endless Passage

Time flows softly, a river untamed,
Whispers of moments, aches unclaimed.
In the currents, memories slide,
Lamenting the passage where dreams abide.

Ghostly echoes of laughter ring,
Each heartbeat, a sorrowful sting.
Yet in the shadows, a light does gleam,
Cradling hopes in a fragile dream.

Lonely footsteps on pathways worn,
Carrying burdens, souls forlorn.
Every tick of the clock a tale,
Waves of longing, an endless sail.

Glimmers of love in the fleeting past,
Fleeting glories that fade so fast.
In the lament, a truth takes flight,
Embracing darkness, yearning for light.

Through the passage, we wander and weep,
Beneath the stars, secrets we keep.
In the lament of time's gentle flow,
We find the strength to rise and grow.

Lurking in the Winding Aisles

In shadows deep where whispers weave,
A tangle of thoughts, we dare believe.
Among the shelves where secrets hide,
Old stories linger, side by side.

Every corner bends with time's embrace,
A dance of silence, a hidden place.
Footsteps echo, soft and low,
Lost in the rhythm, we ebb and flow.

The old wood creaks, the candles flicker,
In the heart of night, the moments quicker.
A dusty tome, a ghostly sight,
Calls out softly in the fading light.

With every turn, the air grows thick,
A labyrinth spun, a fateful trick.
Curiosity tugs as we roam,
Each winding aisle, a world called home.

What mysteries wait in the darkened nooks?
Piled high with pages, like those old books.
Here in the quiet, fear takes flight,
Lurking tales in the soft moonlight.

A Journey Through the Twilight Tangles

Beneath a sky of muted hues,
We tread on paths where dreams infuse.
Twilight whispers secrets low,
In tangled woods where shadows grow.

With every step, the world unfolds,
A tapestry of whispers untold.
The air is thick with sweet perfume,
Guiding our hearts through the gathering gloom.

Stars begin to pierce the veil,
As twilight's song begins to sail.
In every rustle, a tale resides,
Of fleeting moments where magic hides.

The breeze carries echoes of the night,
Where branches dance in silvery light.
We lose ourselves in twilight's grace,
A journey captured in time and space.

And as we wander, we start to see,
The beauty held in mystery.
In tangled realms, we find our way,
Through fading dusk into break of day.

The Soft Call of the Cryptic Trail

In moonlit glades where shadows play,
A winding path leads us away.
The whispers of the night take hold,
As secrets unravel, daring and bold.

Each step we take reveals the signs,
Of ancient tales in twisted pines.
A call so gentle, pure and clear,
Draws us closer to what we fear.

Beneath the stars, the forest sings,
Of lost adventures and hidden things.
The trail unfolds like a scroll of dreams,
We navigate by silver beams.

As silence wraps us in its shroud,
We stumble forth, humble, unbowed.
The cryptic path leads us in trust,
To the heart of the world, where dreams combust.

And in the end, what shall we find?
A mirror of the soul refined.
On this soft call, we will prevail,
Eternally bound to the cryptic trail.

Sighs of the Ageless Conundrum

In the realm where thoughts collide,
Whispers echo, secrets reside.
The weight of time, a heavy load,
In shadows cast, our truths corrode.

Mysteries dance like flickering flames,
Each heartbeat carries ancient names.
The fabric of fate, so finely spun,
Unraveling softly 'neath the sun.

Questions linger, like soft refrains,
Sighs of the past in whispered chains.
In the labyrinth of mind, we roam,
Searching for solace, yearning for home.

What answers lie in the fading light?
In the stillness before the night?
The ageless conundrum, an endless quest,
Where every choice is but a test.

In every sigh, the cosmos hums,
A longing deep, as resolution comes.
With open hearts, we seek to know,
The sighs that guide us, ebb and flow.

Refuges in the Shadowed Passage

In the shadows where silence dwells,
Whispers of lost dreams softly swell.
The air is thick with untold tales,
Dust settling where memory pales.

A flicker of light guides the way,
Through tangled roots where shadows play.
Each step echoes the paths once crossed,
In the heart of darkness, nothing's lost.

Underneath the ancient trees,
Secrets float on the gentle breeze.
Time stands still in this sacred space,
Finding refuge, a gentle embrace.

Echoes of laughter float through the night,
Casting away the remnants of fright.
Here in the dim, the soul can breathe,
In the passage, one learns to believe.

So linger a moment, let go of strife,
In the shadows, rediscover life.
An oasis of peace in the twilight glow,
Refuges found where the wildflowers grow.

The Web of Inexorable Paths

Threads of silver interlace the night,
Drawing us close, a mesmerizing sight.
In the fabric of fate, we are entwined,
Every turn, every choice, redefined.

Through winding roads and twisted lanes,
We chase the dreams that ease our pains.
Each step forward, a leap of faith,
In a world that sways, we find our place.

The stars above gleam with intent,
Guiding the hearts with their soft lament.
In every heartbeat, the rhythm plays,
Chasing the light through the darkest days.

Bound by the fates we cannot flee,
Finding strength in what's meant to be.
In this web, where destinies meet,
Every moment, a delicate feat.

With every step, a story unfolds,
In the dance of life, there are tales untold.
So follow the threads and learn to see,
The beauty within this mystery.

Threads of Fate in the Dim Spiral

In the spiral of time, where shadows blend,
Threads of fate twist, converge, and bend.
Each moment a stitch in the vast unknown,
Weaving our stories in whispers, not stone.

The dance of the stars over silent ground,
In every heartbeat, a secret is found.
We journey onward through light and dark,
Embracing the whispers that ignite a spark.

Spools of destiny, run wild and free,
Entwined in the fabric of you and me.
Each loop and knot tells a tale of grace,
In the dance of fates, we find our place.

Look to the night, where the cosmos gleam,
Hope ignites like a distant dream.
In threads of fate, we dare to trust,
Creating our paths from ashes and dust.

So follow the spiral, embrace the ride,
Trust in the journey, let passion guide.
For within the dim, new worlds arise,
In the threads of fate, the heart never lies.

Chronicles of the Unending Walk

With each step forward, stories unfold,
Chronicles written in whispers bold.
The ground beneath tells of paths we've tread,
In echoes of footsteps, our lives are spread.

Mountains we climbed, valleys that swayed,
Through laughter and tears, memories stayed.
Each turn a lesson, each pause a breath,
In the journey of life, there's beauty in depth.

So gather your dreams as you tread the way,
In the chronicles of life, let your heart sway.
For every wanderer knows the song,
In the unending walk, we all belong.

Stars overhead guide our silent quest,
Reminding us always to seek and to rest.
In every horizon, a promise awaits,
In chronicles written by curious fates.

So walk on boldly, embrace every mile,
In the dance of the journey, find your own style.
For the path may twist, but never stray far,
In chronicles endless, you're the shining star.

Reflections in the Labyrinthine Twilight

In the soft glow of fading light,
Shadows dance, secrets take flight.
Whispers echo through twisted ways,
Guiding hearts to the end of days.

Mirrors crack, revealing sight,
Lost in thoughts, fading from night.
Time stands still within this maze,
Each step forward, a lingering gaze.

Glimmers fade as twilight breaks,
Silent truths in silence wakes.
Paths converge, then diverge so fast,
Holding dreams of a distant past.

Veils of dusk conceal the fear,
Yet in shadows, there's a tear.
Voices call in the quiet chill,
Drawing near, against the will.

Beneath the twilight's mystic spell,
Each heart knows its tale to tell.
In the maze where echoes breath,
Reflections linger, life and death.

The Riddle of the Spiraling Depths

Down the spiral, voices hum,
Whispers weave where shadows come.
Secrets fold in the silent night,
Drawing souls with their ancient light.

Every turn a choice to make,
Riddles dance like rippling lake.
Darkness swirls with a knowing grin,
The journey starts where thoughts begin.

Within these depths, a treasure lies,
Wisdom hidden beneath the skies.
Round and round, the echoes sing,
Truth unveiled can often sting.

Lost in circles, some may stray,
Yet each path will find its way.
The heart holds keys to unlock doors,
Among the depths, adventure soars.

Spiraling deeper into the void,
Amongst the fears once deployed.
At the core, a light remains,
Guiding lost souls through the chains.

Voices from the Hidden Corridors

In the halls where echoes dwell,
Voices rise, a timeless spell.
Secrets linger in the air,
Stories whisper, truths laid bare.

Through the cracks of ancient stone,
Shadows drift, though they stand alone.
Every turn brings forth a sigh,
Hidden dreams that long to fly.

Footsteps softly mark the ground,
In these corridors, love is found.
Flickering lights guide the way,
Into the night, where hopes sway.

Trapped in time, yet free to soar,
Voices beckon from each door.
Harmonies of lost desire,
Kindled here, a heart's own fire.

As whispers weave a gentle tune,
Hidden corridors hum to the moon.
In their depths, we claim our fate,
Through the silence, we await.

The Enigma Beneath the Stars

Starry night holds a secret bright,
In the cosmos, dreams take flight.
Threads of fate weave in the sky,
Mysteries hide in the soft sigh.

Galaxies spin in a cosmic dance,
Inviting souls to take a chance.
Each twinkling light, a story spun,
Whispering tales of what's to come.

Beneath the stars, the heart can roam,
Finding paths that lead us home.
Voyagers lost in the vast expanse,
Yearning for fate's sweet entrance.

In eclipsed shadows, truths confide,
A riddle stands beneath the tide.
Questions linger where starlight beams,
Awakening long-forgotten dreams.

As dawn breaks with a gentle sigh,
The enigma fades, but never dies.
Each star a note in the song of night,
Guiding our hearts toward the light.

Spiral Echoes in a Forgotten Quest

In shadows cast by ancient trees,
Whispers linger on the breeze.
A path that winds, a tale untold,
In echoes lost, the heart grows bold.

Footsteps trace forgotten lore,
Secrets knocking at the door.
The quest unfurls, the journey long,
With every step, we find the song.

Stars above, they gently gleam,
Guiding hearts through eroded dream.
In alleys dim, the spirits dance,
While shadows weave a mystic chance.

Courage found in silent night,
Lost desires come to light.
Each turn reveals a new embrace,
In twilight's glow, we find our place.

For in the spiral, life unfolds,
Not just in dreams, but tales of old.
A quest unbroken, time will mold,
In echoes deep, we are consoled.

The Unfurling of the Timeless Path

In the hum of dawn's first light,
Roads unfurl, the heart takes flight.
Steps align with purpose clear,
Each moment draws the soul near.

The whispers of the waking day,
Guide the lost along the way.
With every footfall, time expands,
A dance that life forever spans.

Leaves above in vibrant hue,
Channel warmth, embrace the blue.
Every turn a chance to grow,
Within the flow, we learn to know.

Beneath the sky, wide and vast,
Stories linger from the past.
A path unearths what's yet to come,
In silence, life plays its drum.

Through valleys deep and mountains high,
We wander forth, we touch the sky.
In this unfurling, truths will show,
Timeless paths where spirits flow.

Stories Woven in Faint Light

In shadows soft, the tales begin,
Woven threads of loss and kin.
Faint light flickers, whispers glide,
Through fragile hearts, our dreams abide.

Each silence hums a secret song,
Where moments lost feel more than long.
A tapestry of hopes and fears,
In woven whispers, we shed tears.

The night enfolds, a canvas wide,
Stories linger, hearts collide.
In moonlit beams, the past unwinds,
While destiny in silence binds.

Prompted by the stars above,
Faint echoes pulse with wanting love.
Every glance, a memory kissed,
Within the light, we still exist.

For woven stories lead us true,
To find ourselves, to start anew.
In subtle light, our visions share,
A dance of souls, a breath of air.

Whirls of Fate in Obscured Traffic

In the rush of city's breath,
Whirls of fate will challenge death.
Rivers flow through concrete sets,
Where dreams collide, the heart bets.

Each moment holds a chance to sway,
Paths entwined in bright dismay.
The pulse of life, a frantic pace,
In obscured lanes, we find our grace.

Echoes ring of laughter near,
Through vehicular whirls we steer.
A tapestry of dreams and strife,
In every corner, flickers life.

Red lights pause the fleeting chance,
Time reveals its intricate dance.
The world spins fast, we contemplate,
Amidst the noise, we navigate.

In city's rhythm, fate will hum,
Stories crafted, journeys come.
Through traffic's maze, we find the way,
Whirls of fate in night and day.

9 781805 612919